1 - E - 9
2 - E - 8
3 - E 1
4 - H - 8
5 - H - 2
6 - G - 2
7 - G - 6
8 - E - 1
9 - A - 1
10 - B - 8
11 - C - 2
12 - G - 5
13 - G - 6
14 - F - 1
15 - E - 3
16 - A - 1
17 - I - 6
18 - F - 6

19 - H - 6
20 - F - 8
21 - G - 8
22 - B - 9
23 - G - 5
24 - G - 1
25 - E ?
26 - H
27 - ?
28 - F - 9
29 - 1 - 8
30 - H - 8

8 - 8
4 - 9
6 - 1's
3 - 2's
6 - 6's
1 - 3
2 - 5's

Create a Home Theater Like the Pros. Watch the video on AOL Home.

FINDING YOURSELF
ON THE
ENNEAGRAM

LORETTA BRADY, M.A., M.S.W.

With Illustrations by Dick Trimarco

ThomasMore®
A Division of
RCL • Resources for Christian Living™

Allen, Texas

Send all inquiries to:
Thomas More®
A division of RCL • Resources for Christian Living™
200 East Bethany Drive
Allen, Texas 75002-3804

Toll Free: 800–264–0368
Fax: 800–688–8356

Printed in the United States of America

ISBN 0–88347–336–4

1 2 3 4 5   01 00 99 98 97

CONTENTS

ACKNOWLEDGMENTS

This book has been enriched by contributions from so many people. Dick Trimarco and I created the images you will see here but with a great deal of help. We began with the basic aspects of each Enneagram type. Then we collected real-life, firsthand contributions from many people in various groups which I have led through the Enneagram process. I would turn their contributions into concepts and words. Then Dick would turn them into pictures. Later, after testing out our creations we refined them to come even closer to what each person had said would best reflect their Enneagram numbers. Dick would literally go back to the drawing board again and again. When we felt our creations were complete, they were tested with other people who had not yet learned the Enneagram theory. After completing the process, these people later learned the theory and identified their numbers. We were then able to see an incredibly high reliability in the results. The research continues, as many more people try this new process.

We wish to thank all those people in the Enneagram groups who have made this book possible. Special thanks also to John Powell, S.J., for his tireless editing and supportive encouragement; to Delia, Maria and Sheila Stowe who gave generously of their unique design talents; to all the members of the Stowe family and the Rathjen family for their endlessly creative suggestions; and especially to Bernice Trimarco for her unlimited patience in sensing the needs of both author and illustrator.

——*Loretta Brady*

Introduction

The Enneagram theory of personality suggests there are nine different types or styles of expressing our humanity. The word Enneagram is Greek for "nine points," as in vantage points. The theory describes nine different vantage points from which we each view reality. From these nine views of reality flow all our motivations, our thoughts, our feelings and our choices of action. In each of life's situations, if we look closely, we can see the difference in one person's view from another's.

In Enneagram terms, to know which number we are is to discover the way we view reality. Once this is apparent, we can begin to move beyond crippling patterns in our behaviors. We can move toward growth and greater health. We also can better understand and interact with others. For those interested in self-awareness and growth, the first step of the Enneagram journey, then, is to identify which of the nine types you are. This book is not about the Enneagram theory itself. Nor is it about how to use the Enneagram for your own journey of growth.* This book was created solely for helping you find the Enneagram number that indicates your personality type.

This is a very different approach to identifying your Enneagram number or type than the quizzes and inventories that have been used lately in the field. While a great deal of work has gone into each of those, I have found trouble in using them because of semantic differences. Words mean

---

* I have three other publications which address those topics: *The Enneagram: A Guide to Know Yourself and Understand Others* (Video series-Thomas More); *Beginning Your Enneagram Journey* (Thomas More) and *Awakening to Your LifeGrowth Journey.*

Loretta Brady

different things to different people. I kept asking myself: What would better clarify the essence of each number? I have continually asked people who have found their Enneagram number: How did you discover yours? The answer almost always involved an encounter with people of that number who were displaying the same attributes in live interaction. "When I saw that one person and noticed how he interacted, I knew those would be my same feelings. That's exactly what I would think. That's just how I would look at the situation. That would be my response."

My conclusion to this live research was that people needed a way to "see and experience" firsthand how persons of each Enneagram number might respond to life as it is in process. I have offered opportunities to listen to living examples, groupings of people of each number. This format provides a discussion of the different numbers but not a live experience of each type. It is also hard to organize and limited to those who can attend. Most importantly, it can often be misleading. When those who have misidentified themselves speak with authority on the number they have incorrectly identified, they can confuse those listening.

I wanted to create, in book form, the closest thing to a live presentation of types but with an accuracy that would prevent confusion. It needed to be something that would provide a visual perception suggesting each number. So this book offers a novel way for new Enneagram learners to experience the live energy of each of the nine numbers. Various life situations are described. Then we see how each of the nine Enneagram types responds in their varying ways. The types are represented by figures in real-life action. Matching your imagined response with the figures shown in this book will help you find your number. It will also help you learn about and appreciate the differences of other types of people.

In Enneagram circles, we frequently find an irresistible urge to "type" others. There is something in many of us that likes to tell other people who we think they are. No matter how often we are cautioned not to do this, it still happens. It may be fun. It may be quick and appear efficient. It may seem to be helpful. We may even get a sense of power from it. But we never really do a favor for the other person. The Enneagram process is meant to be a journey of self-discovery. What we are trying to find is a part of ourselves that we have somehow lost. A commonly used analogy is that we have fallen into a trance and have forgotten who we really are. We are like people who have amnesia. It will not help us to remember if another person comes along and pronounces: "You have been asleep, and I'll tell you what you have missed." We must become aware of the sleep we are in and stir ourselves back into wakeful living. This cannot be done quickly or by someone other than us. Another person can only give us his or her inter-pretation. We must take the time needed, have patience with ourselves, and make it a do-it-yourself-observation process. And it still can be enjoyable.

So you will be doing the search yourself. It will take some time. And your essential tool will be self-observation. This tool will help you to uncover layer after layer of your personality until you begin to recognize your own repeating patterns of behavior, your recurrent feelings, your habitual way of thinking, and the underlying motivation for all these. The process will help bring all the parts of you back together. As you begin to stir from the sleep or trance of self-forgetfulness you will experience a self-remembering. You will come alive in a new way. The very process of finding your Enneagram number is an essential part of the whole life journey.

This book does not offer a quiz, a test, an analysis, or an inventory. The design is intended to reach us through all forms of the learning process. It awakens our visual capacities through pictures. It provides a kinesthetic approach by inviting us to experience life. It stimulates emotions and asks for a response from the part of us that seeks emotional expression.

Most importantly, it consistently requires that we observe ourselves in process. It is an entirely new way to go about identifying your Enneagram number through a multi-faceted use of self-observation.

GUIDELINES FOR USING
THE BRADY ENNEAGRAM IDENTIFIER
(THE BEI)

You can

- Go through the process yourself.

- Go through the process with a good friend or therapist.

    This should be someone who knows you very well, cares about you, can be honest with you, and who allows you the final say.

- Or, go through the process alone and also ask a good friend to go through it alone answering how you might answer. Then the two of you compare your results. In the end, you must make the final determination.

- Don't be concerned that you are fitting yourself into a box. Hopefully, you will find your Enneagram number, but there is great variety even within each number. Your individuality won't be threatened by this process.

- In many of the examples, the situation described will evoke negative behavior choices. All the responses will appear to be less than what we imagine our ideal selves to be. If we are honest in our self-observation, we will see our true selves in all shades of light. Some will be less flattering than others. The key to real self-awareness is honest self-observation.

Loretta Brady

- No Enneagram number is better or worse than the others. They each represent a different way to view reality. All have equal possibilities for the most negative behaviors as well as the most positive behaviors. Which way that goes depends on our choices in life, not on our Enneagram numbers.

- The approach of this book involves drawings of people in active life. As you go through the process you will notice both male and female figures. They have been used interchangeably to represent all the numbers since the Enneagram types are not limited to one gender. There are no "female numbers" or "male numbers." All of us—male or female—could be any one of the numbers. As you compare your responses to the figures shown, don't be limited by gender. If a certain figure conveys what would be your response, then choose it, whether male or female.

- Don't look for an exact match. That will be rare. Only seek to find the greatest similarity to you.

- Don't choose who you would like to be, but rather who you actually are—for better or for worse.

Directions for Using
The Brady Enneagram Identifier
(The BEI)

- Before you begin, go to the back of the book and fold out your answer sheet. Then return to this page to continue with directions.

- There are 30 different situations described in the book. You will start by reading about Situation 1.

- Then picture yourself in that situation. Observe yourself. How would you expect to see and hear yourself responding? Take time to think deeply about yourself and your possible reaction to the situation before continuing.

- On the page after each description you will encounter nine figures that dramatize nine different responses to the situation you have just considered. Study the facial expression and body language of each figure. Then, read the words that accompany each figure.

- Ask yourself which of the nine figures comes closest to your imagined response. Remember, it is not likely that you will find an exact match. Just look for the figure closest to how you would have reacted: what you would have thought and felt, done and said in the same situation.

- If you have difficulty identifying with any of the figures, sense the overall energy or essence of each one. (For example: strength, compassion, detachment, delight, pride, frustration, artistry, confusion, relaxation.) Then choose the one that comes closest to your energy or essence.

- Only choose one figure for each of the 30 situations.

- For each situation, record the letter of the chosen figure on your answer sheet at the back of the book.

Sample:

ANSWER SHEET

Situation	Letter	Enneagram Number
1	F	
2	A	
3	H	

- You will be filling in the third column titled Enneagram Number after you have gone through all 30 situations.

- After Situation 30, there are directions for tallying your results. Look at these directions only after you finish reading about all 30 situations and choosing one figure from each.

- Enjoy the process. Your self-observation will gradually bring you greater self-awareness and self-knowledge.

What Is Your Life Motto?

What motto expresses your core motivation or underlying attitude about life?

Beneath all our thoughts, our feelings, and our choices of action lie basic core motivations for life. This is WHY we do what we do.

It's not because someone else said so. We can still freely choose to follow or not.

It's not because of an event. We each react in varying ways to the same event.

It's not because of our upbringings. Sisters and brothers often respond differently to life and its events.

Why we do what we do is because of something in each of us—something that represents what the core of life is for us.

What's the life motto that expresses the core of your behavior?

Remember:

- When you turn the page, don't look for an exact match, just the one most like your response.

- You can choose a male or female figure, regardless of your own gender, whichever figure best conveys your motto.

- Record the letter of your chosen figure on your answer sheet next to Situation 1.

Which of these mottoes best expresses your core motivation or underlying attitude about life?

19

What Is Your Immediate Reaction To An Accident?

Imagine that you and some other people are going to an event together. You are walking toward the entrance of the place where the event is to be held. Take a moment to get a clear picture of this in your imagination.

Suddenly one of you trips on a cracked sidewalk and falls.

Each of you reacts differently to this happening.

What is your first, most instinctive reaction to this occurrence?

There may be many things you would do or say, but what is your first, most immediate response?

Remember:

- Don't try to think of what you should do or what you think might be the right answer. There is no right answer.

- Just be honest in your self-observation.

- When you turn the page, choose the figure that comes closest to representing your first, most immediate response.

- Record the letter of your chosen figure on your answer sheet next to Situation 2.

One person falls on a cracked sidewalk and is hurt. Nine others react in different ways.

What Happens When Your Plans Are Abruptly Changed?

Imagine that you had planned to take a train for a meeting, or to shop, or meet a friend, or attend a concert.

Picture how you would have set up this whole engagement, how you would have arranged things.

Just as you are arriving at the station you see "your" train pulling out.

What do you think? How do you feel?

What do you say? What do you do?

How would you look to someone watching this scene?

Remember:

- On the following page, notice the facial expressions and body language. Read the words.

- Choose the figure that is reacting most like you would—for better or worse.

- Record the letter of your chosen figure on your answer sheet next to Situation 3.

You have just missed a train you had planned to catch.

TO TRAINS
LIMO RENTALS →
TIME IS MONEY. LET'S GET TOGETHER AND RENT A LIMO.
D
HOW DARE THAT TRAIN LEAVE WITHOUT ME.
C
I JUST FEEL THAT I WASN'T MEANT TO GO TODAY.
H
WELL, I GUESS I'LL JUST WAIT FOR THE NEXT TRAIN TO COME.
I
LOUNG

How Do You React To Other People When They Are The Cause Of Disrupted Plans?

Imagine that you have prearranged to meet someone. You have set the place and the time with them.

You arrive at the agreed-upon place and in plenty of time for the meeting.

The other person isn't there. You wait. Still no one comes. It is past the time of the meeting. Now what?

What do you think happened? What do you decide to do?

Picture yourself in this situation. Observe your reaction.

Remember:

- Choose the figure that shows the greatest similarity of reaction to yours—male or female.

- Record the letter of your chosen figure on your answer sheet next to Situation 4.

Y ou are waiting for someone who is late for your meeting.

How Do You React When An Uncontrollable Outside Event Changes?

Imagine that you are all dressed and ready to enjoy a beautiful sunny day.

Suddenly, the weather takes a turn. The sky gets cloudy and dark. Rain begins to fall.

How will this affect you, your plans, your mood, your attitude?

Remember:

- Even if this situation evokes negative behavior choices in you—don't judge—just observe.

- Be honest with yourself in your self-observation. Choose the figure who is reacting most like you would.

- Record the letter of your chosen figure on your answer sheet next to Situation 5.

A sunny day suddenly changed to a rainy day.

35

What Causes You To Choose Life Each Day?

In observing yourself in the first moments of wakefulness, what begins to stir you to get up and out of bed?

Don't limit your answer to outside agents like the alarm clock or the boss.

Go deeper than that into your own attitudes about life.

What motivates you each morning to live another day?

Take a few moments with this. Try to isolate the very first inklings or desires that occur to you as inviting enough to get you out of bed.

Remember:

- Don't look for an exact match.

- Choose the figure that best represents your overall attitude toward life.

- Choose a male or female figure, regardless of your own gender.

- Record the letter of your chosen figure on your answer sheet next to Situation 6.

What motivates you to get out of bed in the morning?

Most Of Us At One Time Or Another Have Wished We Had More Money

"I wish I were rich. Then I would . . ."

"If only I had a little extra money, I would . . ."

Imagine what you would do. How would you like to spend that money? What comes to mind just considering this?

Well, what if you won $40 million in the lottery?

What then . . . ?

Remember:

- In looking at each figure, notice the facial expressions, and the body language. Read the words.

- Choose the figure that best reflects your response to this event.

- Record the letter of your chosen figure on your answer sheet next to Situation 7.

You just won 40 million dollars in the lottery.

43

Would You Describe Yourself As An Optimist, A Pessimist, Or Someone In Between?

You probably know the famous question about the half glass of water:

Is the glass half empty or half full?

How would you answer?

Remember:

- It will be unlikely that any of the figures on the next page expresses exactly what you would in response to this question.

- Choose the reaction that comes closest to the same spirit as your response to the question.

- Record the letter of your chosen figure on your answer sheet next to Situation 8.

Is the glass half empty or half full?

47

How Do You Respond To Criticism?

Picture yourself on your way to meet someone you know. When you arrive, you discover that they are waiting for you. Then they greet you with: "You're late!"

The question here isn't whether you are actually late or not. But rather, how do you feel when someone greets you with an accusation?

How do you feel?

What do you think?

What do you say and do?

Remember:

- This example will likely evoke defensive reactions. This is not surprising, merely human.

- To get to know yourself better it is important to be honest with yourself.

- Record the letter of your chosen figure on your answer sheet next to Situation 9.

Someone who is waiting for you greets you by saying: "You're late!"

OH MY GOSH! ARE YOU SURE I'M LATE? I WAS TOLD THIS WATCH WAS GUARANTEED.

B

I'M AWARE OF THAT. HOWEVER, YOUR DIRECTIONS WERE RIDICULOUSLY APPALLING.

A

OW! THAT HURTS! REJECTED EVEN BEFORE I'VE CONNECTED.

E

I'M SO SORRY I KEPT YOU WAITING. I HOPE YOU WON'T HAVE BAD FEELINGS ABOUT ME.

F

51

How Do You Look Ahead To The Future?

Imagine that tomorrow is a free day. No work. No school. No commitments. You can do with it whatever you choose.

How do you start planning ahead what you will do with this free time? Does your planning involve other people or time alone? Does it get very specific or stay pretty loose and general?

Will your free day be filled with play or work—or both?

Do you look forward to an active or passive day?

Get the feel of your habitual way of planning and using free time.

Remember:

- Don't look for an exact match.

- Look for the figure that has the greatest similarity to your approach to free time.

- Record the letter of your chosen figure on your answer sheet next to Situation 10.

SITUATION 10

Tomorrow is a free day. What are your plans?

54

SITUATION 11

How Would You Most Prefer To Help The Less Fortunate?

When we view other people as less fortunate than we are, it's because we see something important missing from their lives.

Presume you are fully talented and could do any job.

What group of people are you most drawn to help? And what would you do for them?

Observe yourself helping a group in some way.

Remember:

- When you turn the page, you will probably not find your specific choice.

- Consider all the figures, whom they are helping, and what they are doing to help.

- Choose the figure that conveys the same sense of purpose as you would hope to have.

- Record the letter of your chosen figure on your answer sheet next to Situation 11.

What's your preferred way to help the less fortunate?

What Kind Of A Leader Would You Be?

Whether you welcome it or not, you've been chosen to lead a group of people.

Observe yourself in this circumstance to identify the approach you would take to leadership.

Remember:

- Look at all the figures on the following page.

- Choose the one whose overall energy, spirit and approach is most similar to yours.

- Record the letter of your chosen figure on your answer sheet next to Situation 12.

What kind of a leader would you be?

Imagine Yourself
On A Fishing Trip

While not all of us would choose to go fishing, let's say you "got an offer you couldn't refuse."

How would you be involved with this experience?

Observe yourself in this imaginary situation.

Remember:

- Study each figure on the following page. Notice their words and body language.

- Get the sense of each person's attitude about being on this trip.

- Choose the one figure—male or female—whose activity and attitude is most like yours would be.

- Record the letter of your chosen figure on your answer sheet next to Situation 13.

I magine yourself on a fishing trip.

B CLOUD COVER, CRYSTAL CLEAR STREAM, FUN AND FRIENDS, THIS IS AS GOOD AS IT GETS.

FISHING IS NOT FOR ME. I COME TO BE WITH THE OTHERS AND MAKE THINGS NICE.

A

I WONDER HOW FISH KNOW WHEN AND WHERE TO SPAWN.

E

I'VE COME PREPARED. I HAVE EVERY ROD, LINE, AND LURE WE MIGHT NEED, JUST IN CASE.

G

OH, IT'S SO SAD THOUGH THAT THIS DAY WILL EVER HAVE TO END.

H

How Would You Respond To Being Fired From Your Job?

Imagine that you are unexpectedly and suddenly fired from your job.

The personnel manager tells you that you are no longer needed. Your abilities are not of value at this time.

Observe how you respond to the personnel manager.

Remember:

- This situation will probably provoke negative reactions and defensive responses. If so, that's natural.

- Be honest with yourself as you compare your imagined response to those shown on the next page.

- Choose the response that comes closest to yours.

- Record the letter of your chosen figure on your answer sheet next to Situation 14.

What is your response to the personnel manager who has just fired you?

Imagine You've Just Had A Car Accident

Your car skidded off the road and into a tree. No one was hurt, but your car is damaged.

Observe your reaction to this accident.

What is the first thing you say or do?

Remember:

- Relate your imagined response to those shown on the next page.

- Choose which figure is reacting most like you would.

- Record the letter of your chosen figure on your answer sheet next to Situation 15.

You've just had an accident with your car.

You've Been Invited To A Pool Party

Whether or not this is your idea of fun, imagine yourself there.

Observe what place you find for yourself in this social setting.

Remember:

- Enjoy the process.

- Check out the figures on the next page to see which activity feels most comfortable to you.

- Record the letter of your chosen figure on your answer sheet next to Situation 16.

SITUATION 16

Where would you be found at an outdoor pool party?

SITUATION 17

You Are Going To Be A Part Of The Production Of A Play

Again, presume you are fully talented and imagine yourself as part of the play's production.

Observe yourself in the job that seems most interesting and appealing to you.

Remember:

- You can choose either male or female figures.

- All the possible options are not represented on the next page.

- Observe the figures there; and see which comes closest to "your" type of job.

- Record the letter of your chosen figure on your answer sheet next to Situation 17.

What job would best suit you in the production of a play?

What Message Would You Want To Hold Up To The World?

Not everyone likes to wear T-shirts with words on them.

But if this were how to get your message across, what would your T-shirt say?

Observe through your imagination what you would write on your T-shirt for the world to view.

Remember:

- The messages on the following page may be more general than yours.

- After reading all nine, which message would convey the greatest similarity to yours?

- Record the letter of your chosen figure on your answer sheet next to Situation 18.

What T-shirt best expresses your message to the world?

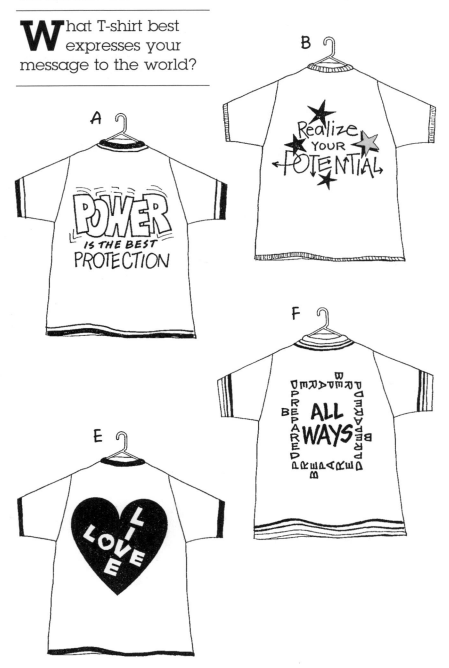

A — POWER IS THE BEST PROTECTION

B — Realize YOUR POTENTIAL

E — LOVE LIVE

F — ALL WAYS BE PREPARED

C — TOGETHER WE CAN FIX WHAT'S WRONG WITH THE WORLD

D — Let the Good Times Roll

G — PEACE HARMONY

H — THE MORE YOU KNOW, THE MORE YOU KNOW YOU DON'T.

87

What Part Do You Like To Play On A Planning Committee?

Imagine that you have been asked to serve on the planning committee for the Olympic Games.

You have the talent to do any job. The key to your self-observation is to identify from your imagination what seems most appealing, or perhaps most enjoyable for you to do.

Remember:

- Check out the figures on the next page to decide which job would most appeal to you.

- Choose a male or female figure, regardless of your own gender.

- Record the letter of your chosen figure on your answer sheet next to Situation 19.

Which job would you do on the Planning Committee for the Olympic Games?

B — I HOPE TO CREATE DRAMATIC CEREMONIES SYMBOLIZING THE UNIQUE SIGNIFICANCE OF THESE OLYMPICS.

A — I'LL GATHER ALL THE INFORMATION AND SET UP THE NEEDED SYSTEMS.

F — I'LL MONITOR EVERYTHING TO BE CERTAIN IT'S DONE RIGHT—ACCORDING TO THE HIGHEST STANDARDS.

E — MY HEART GOES OUT TO THE YOUNG ATHLETES. I'LL MAKE THEM FEEL AT HOME.

First Impressions Count

We all give others a sense of who we are even before we speak.

The way we approach others, our facial expressions, gestures, and body language all speak volumes about who we are.

Imagine meeting someone for the first time.

Observe what first impression of yourself you try to give even before you speak.

Remember:

- The body language is what we hope will best communicate our inner message.

- Carefully study the full spirit and energy of each figure before choosing one.

- Record the letter of your chosen figure on your answer sheet next to Situation 20.

What is the first impression of yourself you want to give people?

95

How Do You Act As You Enter A New Environment?

Imagine you have entered a restaurant. You're seated and getting acquainted with the place and the menu.

What are your most frequent reactions to this type of situation?

Observe yourself in this setting.

What do you notice?

Is the situation pleasant, comfortable, or unpleasant, irritating, frustrating, bewildering, delightful, intolerable, scary or what?

Remember:

- When you look over the figures on the following page there may not be one exactly like you.

- Choose the one who is acting as you most likely would in a restaurant situation like this.

- Record the letter of your chosen figure on your answer sheet next to Situation 21.

What do you usually say or do as you are getting seated and starting to order in a restaurant?

What Do You Find Lacking Most Often In Others?

There is something each of us thinks is a most important quality. And when we find it lacking in others, we tend to be critical of them.

One important way this can be observed is by recalling what our most frequent critical statements are.

Observe yourself in a critical role.

What's the specific quality you seem to be targeting? What do you want to say most of all?

Remember:

- As you study the figures on the next page notice which one you agree with most.

- Choose the figure criticizing in a way most familiar to how you would.

- Record the letter of your chosen figure on your answer sheet next to Situation 22.

When you feel critical toward others, what do you want to say most of all?

103

How Do You Act Or Interact At A Sporting Event?

Some of us get deeply involved in the event.

Others are more involved with the other spectators.

And then there are those of us who are, in various ways, involved with ourselves.

Picture yourself sitting in the stands at a ball game. Observe your particular style.

What are you most likely saying, thinking or shouting?

Remember:

- In looking at the figures on the next page, get a sense of their different energies and focus.

- Choose the one who reminds you most of how you act or interact at these events.

- Record the letter of your chosen figure on your answer sheet next to Situation 23.

A t a sports event, what are you most likely to be heard saying or shouting?

The Way We View Driving Or Riding In A Car Says A Lot About How We View Ourselves, Others, And Life

When you drive or ride in a car, are you

    . . . focused on the driving?

    . . . involved in a sport?

    . . . in a protective mode?

    . . . busy reprimanding?

    . . . focused on people?

    . . . into the fun of it?

    . . . in your head?

    . . . in your feelings?

    . . . into sensations?

Picture yourself as a driver or as a passenger.

Observe what your attitude and your own focus would be.

Remember:

- Either male or female figures can be chosen.

- Choose which figure is most like you on a regular basis.

- Record the letter of your chosen figure on your answer sheet next to Situation 24.

SITUATION 24

What is your attitude about driving?

110

B

C

F

G

How Do You View The Negative Events Of Today's World?

Every day, through radio and TV, in newspapers and magazines—and even in conversation—we hear numerous stories about what is going wrong in our world.

In general how do you react?

What do you think?

How do you feel?

What is your view?

Remember:

- Don't consider how you think you should react, but how you actually do react.

- Each figure on the next page is expressing a different attitude through words, gestures, expressions, and posture. Consider all this when you choose the one most like you.

- Record the letter of your chosen figure on your answer sheet next to Situation 25.

How do you view the negative happenings of today's world?

What Advice Would You Give To Young People Preparing For Adulthood?

We all have enough life experience to pass on something we have learned to others coming along.

We also have certain approaches to life we value most.

Picture yourself responding to a teenager who asks you: What's the most important advice you can give me about life?

Remember:

- This is a fantasy. Most teenagers don't ask for advice.

- Consider the advice given by the figures on the following page. Note both their words and the attitudes they portray before you choose one.

- Record the letter of your chosen figure on your answer sheet next to Situation 26.

What advice would you give to young people preparing for adulthood?

B
DEVELOPE AN ATTRACTIVE RESUMÉ AND NETWORK WITH SUCCESSFUL PEOPLE WHO MAKE THINGS HAPPEN.

A
OBSERVE OTHERS STUDY AND LEARN ALL ABOUT LIFE BEFORE GETTING INVOLVED.

E
YOU SHOULD DO SOMETHING WORTHWHILE WITH YOUR LIFE THAT WILL HELP IMPROVE THE WORLD.

F
DON'T MAKE WAVES. GO WITH THE FLOW. BE PATIENT. LIFE WILL COME TO YOU.

119

All Of Us At Times Suffer "The Slings And Arrows" Of Poor Treatment By Others

Of all the negative ways you might be treated by others, which is the worst?

Which is the most angering, frightening, or most anxiety-producing, the most embarrassing, the most demoralizing—the most difficult way for you to be treated by others?

Sometimes it's hard for us to recall a negative image of ourselves. We would rather not remember. But this situation asks just that:

Recall how you feel, what you say to yourself and how you look when you are the recipient of the worst treatment.

Remember:

- The figures on the following page represent nine different responses to negative treatment from others. Not all things will bother all people.

- Study each figure and notice which one activates the strongest physical or emotional reaction in you.

- Choose the figure whose response grips you the most.

- Record the letter of your chosen figure on your answer sheet next to Situation 27.

What is the worst way for you to be treated by others?

A — IT'S INFURIATING WHEN SOMEONE BLINDSIDES ME.

B — I THOUGHT I HAD PREPARED FOR EVERYTHING. THEN THEY TRICKED ME.

G — WHEN CONFRONTED AND FORCED TO LOOK AT MY OWN PAIN, I FEEL TRAPPED WITH NO ESCAPE, NO OPTIONS, NO FREEDOM.

F — I TRY SO HARD. I CAN'T STAND TO BE CRITICIZED.

Most Of Us Want To Be Seen In A Favorable Light

It follows, then, that we also have an unfavorable light in which we hope never to be seen.

Which way do you hope you will *never* be seen by others?

This situation may be the hardest of all. Here you are being asked to choose a figure that is the total opposite of how you constantly work to portray yourself. This situation shows the image you try hardest to avoid.

Remember:

- Your emotions and physical reactions can indicate a lot about you.

- Observe your reactions as you look over each of the figures on the next page.

- When you come across the one who is expressing most of all "how you never want to be seen," you will probably react in some way. You may even shudder.

- Record the letter of your chosen figure on your answer sheet next to Situation 28.

How do you never want to be seen?

How Do You Want To Be Known—Now And Forever?

We each have certain qualities of which we are very proud. We like it when people notice these and then compliment us.

We want to be known for these characteristics.

In fact, we would probably want what we are proudest of to be carved on our tombstones.

Most of all, what would you want to be carved on your tombstone?

Remember:

- On the next page there are no figures, only tombstones with words.

- The words and the actual design of the burial place are all meant to suggest a special message about you.

- Choose the one that best symbolizes and summarizes your life.

- Record the letter of your chosen figure on your answer sheet next to Situation 29.

Which tombstone would best symbolize and summarize your life?

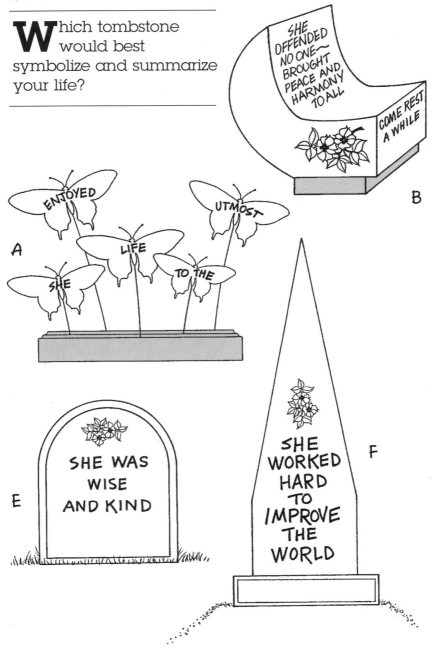

She offended no one ~ brought peace and harmony to all

Come rest a while

B

A

ENJOYED
LIFE
UTMOST
SHE
TO THE

E

SHE WAS
WISE
AND KIND

F

SHE
WORKED
HARD
TO
IMPROVE
THE
WORLD

When Things Are Good, What's Good About Them?

We evaluate in different ways.

In earlier situations, we looked at our different ways of focusing on the negative. Now, let's look at how you focus on the positive.

What are the key ingredients that would make something like this very process we have been going through a positive experience?

Imagine yourself telling a friend about this process. What would you stress or highlight in a positive way?

Remember:

- It is important to read all nine approaches, noting both the words and the body language of the figures.

- Which figure presents something similar to what you might say if you were trying to be positive?

- Record the letter of your chosen figure on your answer sheet next to Situation 30.

- After recording your choice for Situation 30, go on to the directions for tallying final results.

What would you highlight in your positive introduction of this process?

B
IT'S A COMFORTABLE AND PLEASANT WAY TO LOOK AT YOURSELF WITHOUT MUCH BOTHER.

A
IT'S A WONDERFUL WAY TO BECOME MORE COMPASSIONATE TOWARDS OTHERS — AND MYSELF, TOO, I SUPPOSE.

F
THE DIRECTIONS ARE VERY CLEAR. YOU DON'T GET ANXIOUS LIKE YOU DO WITH A TEST.

E
EFFECTIVE, EFFICIENT, COULD BE A VERY SUCCESSFUL PRODUCT FOR WORK, HOME, ANY GROUP.

DIRECTIONS FOR TALLYING
THE RESULTS OF
THE BRADY ENNEAGRAM IDENTIFIER
(THE BEI)

- Be sure you have chosen one, and only one, figure for each of all 30 situations before you begin to process your results.

- A complete correlation chart appears on the following pages.

- With the answer sheet alongside the correlation chart, use the chart to transpose each of your letter answers into an Enneagram number. List the Enneagram numbers in the third column on your answer sheet.

  Sample: <u>ANSWER SHEET</u>

Situation	Letter	Enneagram Number
1	F	1
2	A	1
3	H	2

- After using the correlation chart, count and tally how many times you chose each of the Enneagram numbers.

- Record your tally totals in the area provided at the bottom of the answer sheet.

CORRELATION CHART FOR THE BRADY ENNEAGRAM IDENTIFIER (THE BEI)

SITUATION				_CORRELATIONS_				
1	A-3	B-1	C-4	D-6	E-9	F-2	G-7	H-5	I-8
2	A-2	B-3	C-1	D-7	E-8	F-4	G-6	H-9	I-5
3	A-7	B-2	C-8	D-3	E-1	F-5	G-6	H-4	I-9
4	A-9	B-1	C-4	D-5	E-6	F-2	G-7	H-8	I-3
5	A-4	B-1	C-7	D-9	E-3	F-8	G-6	H-2	I-5
6	A-9	B-3	C-7	D-1	E-6	F-5	G-2	H-8	I-4
7	A-3	B-7	C-1	D-8	E-5	F-2	G-6	H-9	I-4
8	A-9	B-2	C-5	D-4	E-1	F-3	G-8	H-7	I-6
9	A-1	B-6	C-8	D-5	E-4	F-2	G-9	H-3	I-7
10	A-1	B-8	C-3	D-6	E-2	F-4	G-7	H-5	I-9
11	A-8	B-7	C-2	D-9	E-5	F-6	G-1	H-4	I-3
12	A-8	B-2	C-4	D-3	E-9	F-6	G-5	H-1	I-7
13	A-2	B-7	C-1	D-8	E-5	F-9	G-6	H-4	I-3
14	A-3	B-2	C-9	D-6	E-4	F-1	G-5	H-7	I-8
15	A-6	B-1	C-2	D-9	E-3	F-5	G-4	H-8	I-7

(CONTINUED ON PAGE 141)

CORRELATION CHART FOR
THE BRADY ENNEAGRAM IDENTIFIER
(THE BEI)

SITUATION				_CORRELATIONS_				
16	A-1	B-5	C-8	D-4	E-9	F-2	G-6	H-3	I-7
17	A-2	B-4	C-3	D-7	E-8	F-1	G-9	H-5	I-6
18	A-8	B-3	C-1	D-7	E-2	F-6	G-9	H-5	I-4
19	A-5	B-4	C-8	D-9	E-2	F-1	G-7	H-6	I-3
20	A-2	B-1	C-6	D-3	E-7	F-8	G-4	H-9	I-5
21	A-1	B-2	C-3	D-7	E-4	F-5	G-8	H-6	I-9
22	A-4	B-9	C-6	D-3	E-5	F-8	G-7	H-2	I-1
23	A-8	B-2	C-3	D-4	E-6	F-7	G-5	H-1	I-9
24	A-8	B-4	C-2	D-5	E-6	F-9	G-1	H-7	I-3
25	A-4	B-1	C-5	D-3	E-9	F-6	G-2	H-8	I-7
26	A-5	B-3	C-8	D-7	E-1	F-9	G-2	H-6	I-4
27	A-8	B-6	C-5	D-2	E-4	F-1	G-7	H-9	I-3
28	A-6	B-2	C-3	D-8	E-5	F-9	G-1	H-7	I-4
29	A-7	B-9	C-2	D-3	E-5	F-1	G-6	H-4	I-8
30	A-2	B-9	C-7	D-4	E-3	F-6	G-1	H-8	I-5

Interpreting your Results
for
The Brady Enneagram Identifier
(The BEI)

- Check your tally totals. If one Enneagram number has been chosen at least ten times, and more frequently than the others, this indicates you have most likely identified your Enneagram number.

Sample Tally:	1s **0**	2s **2**	3s **0**		
	4s **5**	5s **11**	6s **4**		
	7s **4**	8s **4**	9s **0**		

These results indicate that the person who chose these answers is an Enneagram Number Five.

The results in this sample also show that the Numbers 4, 6, 7 and 8 have some significance as numbers "connected" to the 5.

- THE WINGS:

    Each Enneagram number has two "wing numbers." The wings are the numbers on either side of your Enneagram number, as shown here on the diagram. The wings of each number add some of their flavor and energy to the behavior of the core number. While we always operate from the motivational core of our own number, sometimes we take on the behaviors of these wing numbers. For example, if your Enneagram number is 5, you will probably have some of the

Loretta Brady

behaviors of 4 and 6. That is why you may have chosen some figures from these other numbers, too. But, this is not a necessary result.

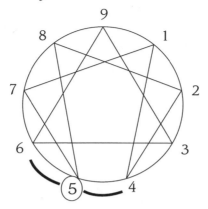

- If your results are unclear you may have identified more strongly with one of your "wings" rather than your core number.

- To give an example of how this might explain your unclear results: For most of the situations you may have chosen Number 5 and Number 7. This could be giving you a clue to consider Number 6 as your core.

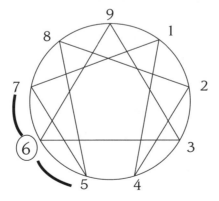

- THE DIRECTIONS:

  Each Enneagram number has two "direction numbers," found at the opposite end of the connecting lines, as shown here on the diagram. The directions are the numbers whose energies we sometimes add to our own at certain times in our lives when we move toward destructive behaviors or toward growthful behaviors. For example, if you are a 5, you may have been inclined at times to choose some of the 7 and 8 behaviors.

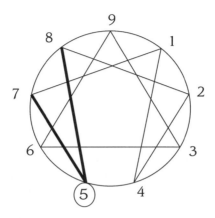

- Again if your results are unclear, you may be identifying with one of your "directions." For example: in most of the situations you may have chosen Number 5 and Number 2. This could be indicating that you are a Number 8 identifying more strongly with your two directions rather than with your core number.

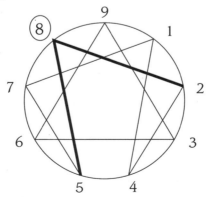

Loretta Brady

- *THE LOOK-ALIKES:*

  There are certain Enneagram numbers that seem to look alike in their behaviors. However, the core of motivation for each is very different. In other words, they may act in similar ways but for different reasons. People sometimes misidentify themselves by focusing on behavior rather than motivation. It is motivation that is the basis for an Enneagram type.

- The following are succinct summaries of the similarities and differences which the look-alike numbers display.

The most common look-alikes are:

	BEHAVIOR	MOTIVATION
#1	Projects elitism.	To be proper and appropriate.
#4	Projects elitism.	To be aesthetically pleasing.
#1	Obeys rules.	To do the right thing.
#6	Obeys rules.	To do what I was told.
#1	Do what's right.	To be good.
#8	Do what's right.	To be just.
#2	Helps people.	To care for others.
#6	Helps people.	To be dutiful and of service.
#2	Attracted to others.	To meet others' needs.
#9	Attracted to others.	To move with others' energy.
#3	Positive & energetic.	To keep accomplishing.
#7	Positive & energetic.	To keep life happy.
#4	Tends to extremes.	To feel all the highs and lows.
#7	Tends to extremes.	To be free for all options.
#5	Sits and reads.	To study and learn.
#9	Sits and reads.	To relax and enjoy the diversion.

Other look-alikes are:

		BEHAVIOR	MOTIVATION
	#2	Aware of image.	To be helpful.
	#3	Aware of image.	To be productive.
	#4	Aware of image.	To be sensitive and different.
	#5	Fit ideas together.	To ponder profundities.
	#6	Fit ideas together.	To prudently prepare.
	#7	Fit ideas together.	To plan possibilities.
	#8	Strongly charged.	To be the strongest force.
	#9	Strongly charged.	To hold down stress.
	#1	Strongly charged.	To fix what is broken.

---

*	#3	Assertive.	To reach the goal.
*	#7	Assertive.	To overwhelm fears with delight.
*	#8	Assertive.	To prevail over all.
*	#4	Withdrawing.	To experience inner emotions.
*	#5	Withdrawing.	To be safe and private with self.
*	#9	Withdrawing.	To avoid conflict with others.
*	#1	Compliant.	To meet internal standards.
*	#2	Compliant.	To meet others' needs.
*	#6	Compliant.	To meet others' expectations.

*These look-alikes are based on Karen Horney's observations.

**	#2	Independent.	To be the one who helps others.
	#5	Independent.	To be self-sufficient.
	#8	Independent.	To be invincible.
	#3	Vacillates.	To be liked by all.
	#6	Vacillates.	To seek approval, avoid blame.
	#9	Vacillates.	To stay peaceful, avoid conflict.
	#1	Unusual.	To know the ideal way.
	#4	Unusual.	To be like no other.
	#7	Unusual.	To be fascinating and fascinated.

Loretta Brady

#1	Structured.	To do it right.
#3	Structured.	To be efficient and productive.
#5	Structured.	To be thorough and deep.
#2	Fun loving.	To enjoy the people.
#7	Fun loving.	To enjoy the experiences.
#9	Fun loving.	To enjoy togetherness.
#4	Passionate.	To intensify each moment.
#6	Passionate.	To guard the truth.
#8	Passionate.	To demand justice.

**The 18 look-alikes above are based on research done by Paul Robb, S.J., and my collaborative study with him, Suzanne Zuercher, O.S.B., and Dick Wright.

- For those of you whose results were unclear, return to your tally totals after reading over these descriptions of the wings, directions, and look-alikes. See if you can find any pattern in your results that will give you a clue as to how you may have misidentified yourself. You may even find your core number.

- If your results still leave you unsure of your core number, take heart. For a large part of our lives we have been in a kind of self-forgetful trance and have lost touch with our true selves. It's understandable that it might take a while to get in touch again. Keep the self-observation process going in your daily life and you will eventually find your Enneagram "home."

Now That I Know My Number What Comes Next?

Once you have identified your Enneagram number, don't rush to change yourself! This is a common temptation.

Finding our Enneagram numbers is just the beginning. The whole journey involves getting reacquainted with our original selves before we became so protective and defensive. At this point in our journey, we need to take time to remember the large and small things that are all a part of us. We need to observe, discover, and reconnect with ourselves.

To start this part of the journey, you may wish to read the short descriptions of each of the Enneagram numbers offered on the following pages. Then I suggest you go on to read my book, *Beginning Your Enneagram Journey.* This book will give you a thorough and grounded introduction. This and other resources for your journey are listed in a bibliography at the end of this book.

Get to know more about the Enneagram theory through books, tapes, and seminars. Learn and experience all you can about your own Enneagram number. Take time with this. Eventually you will want to get to know about your wings and directions. Continue your self-observation to learn more about yourself and where your possibilities for growth lie. At this stage you may want to consult my book, *Awakening To Your LifeGrowth Journey.* The process of growth and change will unfold naturally as you follow this journey.

BRIEF DESCRIPTIONS
OF THE
NINE ENNEAGRAM NUMBERS

Loretta Brady

The core motivation for ONEs is:

In the 30 BEI situations the Enneagram Number ONE figures are:

1-B	2-C	3-E	4-B	5-B	6-D
7-C	8-E	9-A	10-A	11-G	12-H
13-C	14-F	15-B	16-A	17-F	18-C
19-F	20-B	21-A	22-I	23-H	24-G
25-B	26-E	27-F	28-G	29-F	30-G

ONEs' *Idealized Self-Image* or point of pride is:
"I am right and good and self-controlled."

Their *Avoidance* is:
being judged as broken, bad or undisciplined.

For ONEs the *Focus of Energy* is on:
Standards.

IN COMPULSION their anger and resentment about imperfection drives them to push for improvement of self and others.

IN GIFTEDNESS their instinctive sense of goodness helps us all to be our best selves.

The wings of 1 are 9 and 2. The directions of 1 are 4 and 7. A study of these other numbers, too, will enhance your understanding of the Number One.

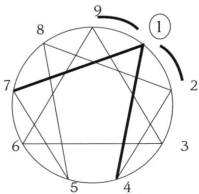

The core motivation for TWOs is:

In the 30 BEI Situations the Enneagram Number Two figures are:

1-F	2-A	3-B	4-F	5-H	6-G
7-F	8-B	9-F	10-E	11-C	12-B
13-A	14-B	15-C	16-F	17-A	18-E
19-E	20-A	21-B	22-H	23-B	24-C
25-G	26-G	27-D	28-B	29-C	30-A

TWOs' *Idealized Self-Image* or point of pride is:
"I care only about you and your needs."

Their *Avoidance* is:
being considered needy or burdensome to others.

For TWOs the *Focus of Energy* is on:
Caretaking.

IN COMPULSION their pride in giving drives them to become indispensable to others.

IN GIFTEDNESS their natural feel for caring and nurturing helps us all to attend to the needs of others and ourselves.

The Wings of 2 are 1 and 3. The Directions of 2 are 4 and 8. A study of these other numbers, too, will enhance your understanding of the Number Two.

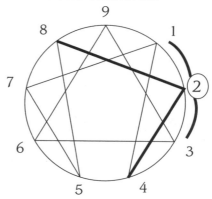

Loretta Brady

The core motivation
for THREEs is:

In the 30 BEI Situations the Enneagram Number THREE figures are:

1-A	2-B	3-D	4-I	5-E	6-B
7-A	8-F	9-H	10-C	11-I	12-D
13-I	14-A	15-E	16-H	17-C	18-B
19-I	20-D	21-C	22-D	23-C	24-I
25-D	26-B	27-I	28-C	29-D	30-E

THREEs' *Idealized Self-Image* or point of pride is:

"I am productive and successful."

Their *Avoidance* is:

being assessed as a failure, a nothing, with no-thing to show.

For THREEs the *Focus of Energy* is on:

Goals.

IN COMPULSION their self-deception drives them to offer an image or a role in place of the real self.

IN GIFTEDNESS their assuring confidence that we can reach our greatest potential helps us all to fully develop our true selves.

The Wings of 3 are 2 and 4. The Directions of 3 are 6 and 9. A study of these other numbers, too, will enhance your understanding of the Number Three.

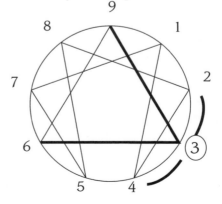

The core motivation
for FOURs is:

BE ALIVE IN THE
TAPESTRY OF LIFE
EXPERIENCED.

In the 30 BEI Situations the Enneagram Number FOUR figures are:

1-C	2-F	3-H	4-C	5-A	6-I
7-I	8-D	9-E	10-F	11-H	12-C
13-H	14-E	15-G	16-D	17-B	18-I
19-B	20-G	21-E	22-A	23-D	24-B
25-A	26-I	27-E	28-I	29-H	30-D

FOURs' *Idealized Self-Image* or point of pride is:
"I am unique. . .different."

Their *Avoidance* is:
being common, ordinary, average, defective.

For FOURs the *Focus of Energy* is on:
Differentness.

IN COMPULSION their envy drives them to mourn what is missing
and want what others have.

IN GIFTEDNESS their sensitivity to uniqueness calls forth the true
inner beauty in all of us, as well as in them.

The Wings of 4 are 3
and 5. The Directions of
4 are 1 and 2. A study of
these other numbers,
too, will enhance your
understanding of the
Number Four.

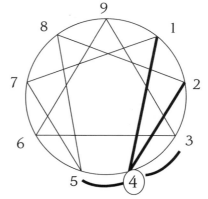

Loretta Brady

The core motivation
for FIVEs is:

IT'S IMPORTANT TO OBSERVE FIRST IN ORDER TO UNDERSTAND REALITY.

In the 30 BEI Situations the Enneagram Number FIVE figures are:

1-H	2-I	3-F	4-D	5-I	6-F
7-E	8-C	9-D	10-H	11-E	12-G
13-E	14-G	15-F	16-B	17-H	18-H
19-A	20-I	21-F	22-E	23-G	24-D
25-C	26-A	27-C	28-E	29-E	30-I

FIVEs' *Idealized Self-Image* or point of pride is:

"I am knowledgeable."

Their *Avoidance* is:

being considered an ignorant fool.

For FIVEs the *Focus of Energy* is on:

Observing.

IN COMPULSION their greediness for knowledge drives them to hold themselves back from others and from life.

IN GIFTEDNESS their wisdom about the essentials of life helps us and them find insightful meaning in everyday living.

The Wings of 5 are 4 and 6. The Directions of 5 are 7 and 8. A study of these other numbers, too, will enhance your understanding of the Number Five.

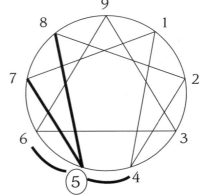

The core motivation for SIXes is:

In the 30 BEI Situations the Enneagram Number SIX figures are:

1-D	2-G	3-G	4-E	5-G	6-E
7-G	8-I	9-B	10-D	11-F	12-F
13-G	14-D	15-A	16-G	17-I	18-F
19-H	20-C	21-H	22-C	23-E	24-E
25-F	26-H	27-B	28-A	29-G	30-F

SIXes' *Idealized Self-Image* or point of pride is:

"I am cooperative, dutiful, loyal and prepared."

Their *Avoidance* is:

being caught in uncertainty or disloyalty.

For SIXes the *Focus of Energy* is on:

Authority.

In Compulsion their fear will drive them to blind obedience or rebellious defiance.

In Giftedness their faith will lead them to step out into life and bring us along with them.

The Wings of 6 are 5 and 7. The Directions of 6 are 3 and 9. A study of these other numbers, too, will enhance your understanding of the Number Six.

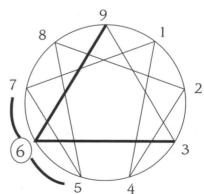

Loretta Brady

The core motivation for SEVENs is:

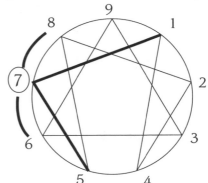

ACCENTUATE THE POSITIVE.

In the 30 BEI Situations the Enneagram Number SEVEN figures are:

1-G	2-D	3-A	4-G	5-C	6-C
7-B	8-H	9-I	10-G	11-B	12-I
13-B	14-H	15-I	16-I	17-D	18-D
19-G	20-E	21-D	22-G	23-F	24-H
25-I	26-D	27-G	28-H	29-A	30-C

SEVENs' *Idealized Self-Image* or point of pride is:
"I am happy and life is terrific."

Their *Avoidance* is:
being trapped in sadness.

For SEVENs the *Focus of Energy* is on:
Experience.

IN COMPULSION their gluttony for experiencing everything will drive them to rush constantly from the threat of sadness to the promise of pleasurable distraction.

IN GIFTEDNESS their joy will help us to celebrate the complete range of real life.

The Wings of 7 are 6 and 8. The Directions of 7 are 1 and 5. A study of these other numbers, too, will enhance your understanding of the Number Seven.

The core motivation for EIGHTs is:

In the 30 BEI Situations the Enneagram Number EIGHT figures are:

1-I	2-E	3-C	4-H	5-F	6-H
7-D	8-G	9-C	10-B	11-A	12-A
13-D	14-I	15-H	16-C	17-E	18-A
19-C	20-F	21-G	22-F	23-A	24-A
25-H	26-C	27-A	28-D	29-I	30-H

EIGHTs' *Idealized Self-Image* or point of pride is:
"I am invincible."

Their *Avoidance* is:
being exposed as vulnerable.

For EIGHTs the *Focus of Energy* is on:
Struggle.

IN COMPULSION their lust for strong excitement drives them to push forcefully toward life.

IN GIFTEDNESS their instinctive sense of innocence helps them to use their power for protection and justice.

The Wings of 8 are 7 and 9. The Directions of 8 are 2 and 5. A study of these other numbers, too, will enhance your understanding of the Number Eight.

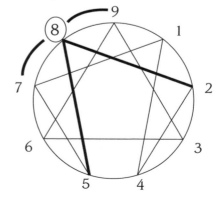

Loretta Brady

The core motivation
for NINEs is:

In the 30 BEI Situations the Enneagram Number NINE figures are:

1-E	2-H	3-I	4-A	5-D	6-A
7-H	8-A	9-G	10-I	11-D	12-E
13-F	14-C	15-D	16-E	17-G	18-G
19-D	20-H	21-I	22-B	23-I	24-F
25-E	26-F	27-H	28-F	29-B	30-B

NINEs' *Idealized Self-Image* or point of pride is:
"I am easygoing, agreeable and peaceful."

Their *Avoidance* is:
being stuck in conflict or discord.

For NINEs the *Focus of Energy* is on:
Stability.

IN COMPULSION their indifference drives them to minimize every-thing.

IN GIFTEDNESS their action in coming to life brings harmony from disparate elements and integration of their own inner selves.

The Wings of 9 are 1 and 8. The Directions of 9 are 3 and 6. A study of these other numbers, too, will enhance your understanding of the Number Nine.

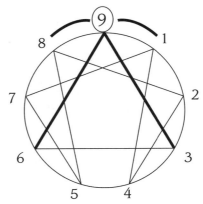

Aspell, Dee Dee and Patrick. *Profiles of the Enneagram: Ways of Coming Home to Yourself.* San Antonio: The Printed Word, 1991.

Baron, Renee and Wagele, Elizabeth. *The Enneagram Made Easy.* San Francisco: Harper, 1994.

Brady, Loretta. *Beginning Your Enneagram Journey.* Allen, TX: Thomas More, 1994.

———. *The Enneagram: A Guide to Know Yourself and Understand Others* (video series). Allen, TX: Thomas More, 1992.

Hurley, Kathleen V. and Theodore E. Dobson. *What's My Type?* San Francisco: Harper, 1991.

Henry, Kathleen. *The Book of Enneagram Prayers.* Jamaica Plain, NY: Alabaster Jar Liturgical Arts, 1987.

Horney, M.D., Karen. *Our Inner Conflicts.* New York: W. W. Norton & Co., 1945.

Kelley, O.C.S., Mary Helen. *Reality in Three Dimensions.* Memphis, TN: Monastery of St. Clare, 1992.

———. *Skin Deep (Designer Clothes by God).* Memphis, TN: Monastery of St. Clare, 1990.

Keyes, Margaret Frings. *Emotions and the Enneagram: Working Through Your Shadow Life Script,* Muir Beach, CA: Molysdatur Publications, 1990.

Metz, Barbara, S.N.D. de N. and John Burchill, O.P. *The Enneagram and Prayer.* Denville, NJ: Dimension Books, 1987.

O'Leary, S.J., Patrick. *Enneagram Basics* (cassette series). Kansas City, MO: Credence Cassettes, 1992.

Palmer, Helen. *The Enneagram: Understanding Yourself and the Others in Your Life.* San Francisco: Harper and Row, 1988.

Riso, Don Richard. *Personality Types: Using the Enneagram for Self-Discovery.* Boston: Houghton Mifflin Company, 1987.

Tart, Charles T. *Waking Up: Overcoming the Obstacles to Human Potential.* Boston: New Science Library, Shambhala, 1986.

Wagner, Jerome P. *The Enneagram Spectrum of Personality Styles.* Portland: Metamorphous Press, 1996.

Wright, Dick. *The Enneagram Triads.* Muir Beach, CA: Molysdatur, 1997.

Zuercher, O.S.B., Suzanne and Dick Wright. *The Enneagram Cards: Sorting Out Your Space.* Notre Dame, IN: Ave Maria Press, 1994.

———. *Enneagram Spirituality: From Compulsion to Contemplation.* Notre Dame, IN: Ave Maria Press, 1991.